LES PETITS PLATS
FRANÇAIS
SIMON & SCHUSTER
ILLUSTRATED

soup cuisine

ANNE-CATHERINE BLEY

Photography by Akiko Ida
Styling by Élodie Rambaud

SIMON &
SCHUSTER
ILLUSTRATED

London · New York · Sydney · Toronto
A CBS COMPANY

English language edition published in Great Britain by
Simon and Schuster UK Ltd, 2011
A CBS Company

Copyright © Marabout 2009

SIMON AND SCHUSTER
ILLUSTRATED BOOKS
Simon & Schuster UK
222 Gray's Inn Road
London WC1X 8HB
www.simonandschuster.co.uk

1 2 3 4 5 6 7 8 9 10

Translation: Prudence Ivey
Copy editor English language: Nicki Lampon

Colour reproduction by Dot Gradations Ltd, UK
Printed and bound in U.A.E.

ISBN 978-0-85720-356-4

Contents

The basics

Cooking

All you need to make soup is a good lidded saucepan, casserole dish, stewpot or decent sized pressure cooker (if you're using a pressure cooker, the cooking time should be halved). You don't even need a non-stick pan; making soup involves a lot of water.

Blending

A food processor is perfect for making thick, smooth soups. But it won't allow you to make a chunky textured soup like gazpacho or borscht.

A hand blender is my favourite method of blending soups. Not only is it very practical, but it can be washed and cleared away very easily and it allows you to get the texture you want.

Storing

Fresh soup will keep for 3–5 days in the fridge depending on the ingredients. Some vegetables, such as cabbage, potatoes and peas, are more volatile and can turn. A soup that has turned has a slightly acidic taste. If this happens, throw it away without hesitation.

Freezing

If you wish to freeze soup, here are some simple rules.

• Divide the soup into small portions (enough for 1 or 2 people) so that you don't have to defrost more than necessary.

• Raw soups (such as gazpacho) cannot be frozen. They contain vegetables (cucumber and peppers) that are full of water. When defrosted, they lose their crunch and the soup will be disgusting.

• Very smooth, thick soups freeze the best.

Frozen vegetables

Frozen vegetables are very good quality and, crucially, are very simple to use. Nothing to peel, chop, crush – it's all done. Nobody can resist that argument! The choice is vast and you can ignore the seasons.

Canned vegetables

Canned vegetables have been somewhat dethroned by frozen, but they remain an option. I use several types, such as chick peas, kidney beans, mushrooms, chestnuts, sweetcorn and tomatoes. Rinse most vegetables well in cold water before using.

Vegetable tips

Cooking though the seasons

Pea soup in December? No problem. Even though fresh peas are only in season in spring and summer, nowadays you can easily find most vegetables throughout the year. However, a new element has to be taken into account: the carbon footprint. Usually the price of fruit and vegetables will depend on the amount of energy needed to get it there on the shelf in front of you. This energy is used to heat greenhouses, wash, peel and chop vegetables, and transport and stock them. Those lovely Kenyan green beans have a prohibitive cost in energy; the courgettes you find throughout winter are no less well-travelled. So, without being extremist and without renouncing everything, the notion of seasonal and local foods should be considered in our grocery choices.

Hints and tips

Garlic: to peel garlic easily, put the cloves in a glass of warm water for 30 seconds. Once peeled, cut in two and remove the shoot.

Chestnuts: to prepare fresh chestnuts, make an incision then scald them for 5 minutes. Peel off the entire husk while they are still warm.

Spinach, sorrel, nettles: fresh spinach needs to be thoroughly washed to get rid of all the dirt. You also need a very large pan as you will probably be cooking large quantities.

Pumpkin, squash: these come in many varieties with many names and shapes. They taste similar and are all delicious. Baby squash are cousins of the pumpkin and have a slight taste of chestnut. They have thick skins that must be scrubbed well and you will need a good knife to cut through it. But you can leave the skin on for cooking and, once cooked, they will blend extremely well.

Lentils, split peas: the recipes in this book use green, yellow or red lentils. You can find them in most supermarkets, as well as split peas. Follow the cooking instructions on the packet.

Leeks: leeks must be washed very thoroughly because earth gets hidden right through to the centre leaves. Cut them in four lengthways and then wash.

Tomatoes: if you can't get fresh, plump, red tomatoes, use any misshapen ones with touches of green or yellow. Or try skinned tinned tomatoes.

Peas: fresh peas are a luxury and you need to shell a great deal to get the right amount for most recipes.

Velvety tomato soup

Preparation time: 10 minutes
Cooking time: 25 minutes
Serves 4

1 tablespoon olive oil
1 onion, finely chopped
2 garlic cloves, crushed
2 tablespoons tomato purée
1 kg (2 lb 4 oz) ripe tomatoes
   (or canned peeled tomatoes),
   washed and chopped
1 bay leaf
a sprig of fresh thyme
a pinch of caster sugar
salt
100 ml (3½ fl oz) single cream

Heat the oil in a large lidded saucepan and lightly brown the onion. Add the garlic, then the tomato purée and the tomatoes.

Tie the bay leaf and thyme sprig together and add to the pan (attach the other end of the string to the edge of the saucepan so you don't forget to remove them before blending). Add the sugar and season with salt.

Add 250 ml (9 fl oz) of water and bring to the boil. Reduce the heat, cover and leave to simmer for 15–20 minutes. Remove the herbs.

Blend the soup. Add the cream, mix well, reheat gently if necessary and adjust the seasoning.

Tomato soup with meatballs

Preparation time: 20 minutes
Cooking time: 25 minutes
Serves 4

Meatballs
100 g (3½ oz) minced beef
2 teaspoons ground cumin
1 small onion, finely chopped
1 egg yolk
1 teaspoon olive oil
salt and freshly ground black pepper

Tomato soup
1 tablespoon olive oil
1 onion, finely chopped
2 garlic cloves, crushed
2 tablespoons tomato purée
1 kg (2 lb 4 oz) ripe tomatoes
  (or tinned peeled tomatoes),
  washed and chopped
1 bay leaf
a sprig of fresh thyme
a pinch of caster sugar
salt
100 ml (3½ fl oz) single cream

Mix the mince, cumin, onion and egg yolk together. Chill in the fridge for at least 15 minutes.

Prepare the tomato soup (follow the recipe on page 8).

Meanwhile, prepare the meatballs, rolling small amounts of meat into balls with your hands.

Heat the olive oil in a frying pan. Add the meatballs and cook well. Season.

Add the meatballs to the soup just after blending and reheat everything for 5 minutes so that the flavours of the meatballs blend with those of the soup.

Tip: Sprinkle a few cumin seeds over the soup as a garnish.

Provençale soup

Preparation time: 15 minutes
Cooking time: 20 minutes
Serves 4

1 tablespoon olive oil
4 garlic cloves, finely chopped
4 shallots, finely chopped
1 red pepper, de-seeded and
    chopped
1 aubergine, peeled and chopped
2 courgettes, peeled and chopped
250 g (8¾ oz) ripe tomatoes (or
    1 small can peeled tomatoes),
    chopped
a sprig of fresh thyme
3 bay leaves
salt and freshly ground black pepper
a bunch of fresh basil
juice of ½ a lemon

Heat the oil in a large saucepan and brown the garlic, shallots and pepper for a few minutes. Add the aubergine, courgettes, tomatoes, thyme and bay leaves and stir. Add 750 ml (26 fl oz) of water and season.

Bring to the boil and then leave to cook over a low heat until all the vegetables are very soft.

Remove the thyme and bay leaves, add the basil and lemon juice and blend so still roughly textured with some vegetable chunks remaining. Reheat gently if necessary and check the seasoning before serving.

Cream of carrot soup

Preparation time: 15 minutes
Cooking time: 35 minutes
Serves 6

3 onions, finely chopped
½ teaspoon ground coriander
1 kg (2 lb 4 oz) carrots, peeled
  and chopped
salt and freshly ground black pepper
100 ml (3½ fl oz) single cream

Brown the onions with the coriander in a large saucepan over a very low heat, stirring occasionally for around 5 minutes until the onions are translucent.

Add the carrots and stir. Add 1.5 litres (2¾ pints) of water and season.

Bring to the boil then reduce the heat and leave to simmer for 25–30 minutes. The carrots should be very tender. Take off the heat and add the cream.

Blend, reheat gently if necessary and check the seasoning.

Four variations on cream of carrot soup

Make the Cream of carrot soup (see page 14), but with the variations as described below...

Carrot, celery and green apple *(top left)*
Don't add the cream – this soup is a little acidic. Use only 700 g (1 lb 9 oz) of carrots and add 3 peeled and cored apples and 2 celery sticks, all cut into pieces. Reserve a little celery to garnish, cooking the remainder with the carrots and apples.

Carrot and orange *(bottom left)*
Do not add the cream. Add 250 ml (9 fl oz) of orange juice just before blending and a little orange zest before serving.

Carrot and coriander *(top right)*
Finely chop the leaves from a bunch of fresh coriander. Add before serving.

Carrot and cumin *(bottom right)*
Brown 1 teaspoon of cumin seeds with the onions. Sprinkle a few extra seeds over the soup before serving.

Pumpkin soup

Preparation time: 15 minutes
Cooking time: 30 minutes
Serves 6

2 teaspoons olive oil
2 onions, chopped
1 garlic clove, chopped
1.2 kg (2 lb 12 oz) pumpkin (will give
 around 800 g pumpkin
 flesh), peeled, de-seeded and
 cut into pieces
salt
100 ml (3½ fl oz) single cream
grated nutmeg

Heat the oil in a large saucepan or casserole dish and cook the onions and garlic for a few minutes until the onions are translucent.

Add the pumpkin, 500–750 ml (18–26 fl oz) of water and a little salt (the pumpkin has a high water content so the pieces don't need to be covered by the water but must be stirred in once or twice during cooking). Bring to the boil then reduce the heat and leave to cook until the pumpkin is tender (around 20 minutes).

Set aside a little of the cooking water, then blend the soup until smooth. Add as much of the reserved water as necessary back into the soup to obtain the right consistency.

Add the cream, reheat gently if necessary, add a little grated nutmeg and check the seasoning.

Four variations on pumpkin soup

Make the Pumpkin soup (see page 18) but with the variations as described below…

Pumpkin and avocado *(top left)*
Once the soup is blended, add 1 avocado cut into pieces. You could also add a few drops of Tabasco sauce.

Pumpkin and coconut milk *(bottom left)*
Add a small piece of peeled and finely chopped fresh ginger and 1 teaspoon of cinnamon and cook with the onions and garlic. After blending, add 110 ml (4 fl oz) of coconut milk in place of the cream. Blend again and season to taste before serving.

Pumpkin and cinnamon *(top right)*
Add 2 teaspoons of cinnamon to the onions at the start of cooking. Sprinkle with a touch of cinnamon to serve.

Pumpkin and chestnut *(bottom right)*
Pierce 500 g (1 lb 1½ oz) of whole chestnuts and boil for 5 minutes. Peel. Cook in a covered pan with a little salted water for 10–15 minutes. Set aside a few chestnuts for decoration. Make and blend the pumpkin soup then add the hot chestnuts and blend roughly. Add the remaining pieces of chestnut before serving.

Squash soup with bacon

Preparation time: 15 minutes
Cooking time: 25 minutes
Serves 6

2 teaspoons olive oil
2 onions, finely chopped
1 kg (2 lb 4 oz) squash, scrubbed,
  de-seeded and cut into pieces
salt and freshly ground black pepper
150 g (5¼ oz) bacon
100 ml (3½ fl oz) single cream
grated nutmeg

Heat the oil in a large saucepan and sweat the onions for a few minutes.

Add the squash and 1 litre (1¾ pints) of water and season. Bring to the boil then reduce the heat and leave to cook until the squash is very tender (around 20 minutes).

Meanwhile, grill the bacon until crispy. Set aside.

Blend the soup until smooth. Add the cream, reheat gently if necessary, add a little grated nutmeg and check the seasoning.

Add the grilled bacon to each bowl just before serving.

Tip: When squash are in season and very ripe, it is not necessary to add the cream as the squash will be creamy enough.

Broccoli soup

Preparation time: 15 minutes
Cooking time: 30 minutes
Serves 6

400 g (14 oz) broccoli, broken into
   florets
100 g (3½ oz) shallots, chopped
100 g (3½ oz) carrots, peeled
   and cut into small pieces
200 g (7 oz) potatoes, peeled
   and cut into small pieces
salt and freshly ground black pepper
100 ml (3½ fl oz) single cream
chopped fresh flat leaf parsley,
   to garnish (optional)

Put all the vegetables into a large, lidded, heavy-based saucepan with 1.2 litres (2 pints) of water. Season. Cover and leave to cook for around 30 minutes. All the vegetables should be very well cooked.

Away from the heat, blend until smooth and add the cream. Reheat gently if necessary and check the seasoning.

Add a little chopped parsley before serving, if using.

Variation: Just before blending, add 8 triangles of Dairylea or similar soft cheese. The melted cheese will replace the cream.

Spinach soup with a poached egg

Preparation time: 10 minutes
Cooking time: 40 minutes
Serves 4

1 tablespoon olive oil
2 shallots, finely chopped
500 g (1 lb 2 oz) spinach, washed
125 g (4½ oz) sorrel leaves, washed
salt and freshly ground black pepper
a pinch of grated nutmeg
100 ml (3½ fl oz) single cream
2 tablespoons white vinegar
4 eggs

Heat the oil in a large lidded saucepan over a low heat. Add the shallots and soften for around 5 minutes.

Add the spinach and sorrel and sweat for a few minutes.

Add 1 litre (1¾ pints) of water and season. Cover and leave to cook over a low heat for around 25 minutes.

Remove from the heat. Add the nutmeg and cream. Blend until smooth, reheat gently if necessary and check the seasoning.

In a saucepan, bring another 1 litre (1¾ pints) of water to the boil with the vinegar. Break the eggs one by one into a ladle then slip them into the boiling water.

Remove the saucepan from the heat and leave the eggs to poach for 3 minutes. Remove the eggs from the water and drain.

Place 1 egg in each bowl of soup and serve.

Cauliflower soup with blue cheese

Preparation time: 10 minutes
Cooking time: 20 minutes
Serves 4

2 teaspoons olive oil
1 onion, finely chopped
500 g (1 lb 2 oz) cauliflower,
  broken into florets
500 ml (18 fl oz) milk
salt and freshly ground black pepper
200 g (7 oz) blue cheese

Heat the oil in a large saucepan or casserole dish and soften the onion over a low heat until translucent.

Add the cauliflower, milk and 500 ml (18 fl oz) of water. Season lightly (the cheese will be salty), bring to the boil and leave to simmer over a low heat for around 10 minutes. Cut three-quarters of the cheese into large chunks.

Away from the heat, add the chunks of cheese. Blend until smooth, reheat gently if necessary and check the seasoning.

Crumble the rest of the cheese into smaller pieces and sprinkle over the bowls of soup just before serving.

Cabbage, chestnut and bacon soup

Preparation time: 10 minutes
Cooking time: 25 minutes
Serves 6

200 g (7 oz) carrots, peeled and
  chopped
800 g (1 lb 12 oz) Savoy cabbage,
  white core removed and leaves
  chopped
500 g (1 lb 2 oz) canned chestnuts
300 g (10½ oz) smoked bacon,
  cut into strips
1 teaspoon olive oil
salt and freshly ground black pepper

Place the carrots in a large saucepan
or casserole dish with 1.2 litres
(2 pints) of water and season lightly.

Bring to the boil, then reduce the
heat and add the cabbage and
chestnuts. Cook for a further
20 minutes.

Meanwhile, fry the bacon strips in
the oil until crisp. Set aside.

Once the carrots are soft, remove
from the heat. Blend very roughly,
add the bacon and serve.

Tip: This soup does not need a lot
of seasoning as the bacon will give
it a salty, smoky flavour.

Puy lentil soup

Preparation time: 5 minutes
Cooking time: 45 minutes
Serves 4

2 tablespoons olive oil
2 onions, finely chopped
250 g (8¾ oz) Puy lentils
salt and freshly ground black pepper
juice of a lemon

Heat 1 tablespoon of the oil in a large saucepan and soften the onions over a low heat.

Once the onions are translucent, rinse the lentils and add to the pan with 1 litre (1¾ pints) of water. Season. Cook over a low heat for 40 minutes until the lentils are well cooked.

Remove from the heat and blend for at least 4–5 minutes until the lentil skins are fully broken up.

Add the lemon juice and remaining olive oil. Reheat gently if necessary and season to taste.

Tip: Nothing is simpler to cook than lentils. Although they take a while to cook (and that really is the only problem) the result is a real treat.

Four variations on Puy lentil soup

Make the Puy lentil soup (see page 32) but with the variations as described below...

Puy lentil and bacon *(top left)*
Keep aside half the onions and fry with 300 g (10½ oz) of smoked bacon, cut into strips, and 1 tablespoon of olive oil. Add once the soup has been blended. Be careful not to add too much salt to the soup as the bacon will be salty enough. Do not add the extra olive oil or the lemon juice when blending.

Curried Puy lentil *(bottom left)*
Mix 1 tablespoon of curry powder with the onions at the start of cooking.

Puy lentil and sausages *(top right)*
Cook 1 sausage with the lentils. Remove the sausage before blending. Cut into small pieces and add to each bowl of soup before serving. Season with care as the sausage will add salt, and leave out the extra olive oil and lemon juice when blending.

Puy lentil and coriander *(bottom right)*
After blending the soup, add roughly chopped leaves from a bunch of fresh coriander and 2–3 chopped fresh mint leaves.

Red lentil soup with coconut milk and lime

Preparation time: 5 minutes
Cooking time: 40 minutes
Serves 4

1 tablespoon olive oil
1 large onion, finely chopped
1 garlic clove, finely chopped
1 teaspoon ground cumin
½ teaspoon ground cinnamon
200 g (7 oz) red lentils
300 g (10½ oz) canned peeled
  tomatoes
salt and freshly ground black pepper
100 ml (3½ fl oz) coconut milk
juice of a lime

Heat the oil in a large saucepan and cook the onion, garlic and spices over a low heat for around 5 minutes.

Add the lentils and tomatoes. Stir well and add 1 litre (1¾ pints) of water. Season.

Bring to the boil then reduce the heat to low and leave to cook for around 30 minutes, stirring occasionally, until the lentils are completely cooked.

Away from the heat, add the coconut milk and lime juice. Blend until smooth, reheat gently if necessary and check the seasoning. Serve.

Red lentil and spinach soup

Preparation time: 10 minutes
Cooking time: 35 minutes
Serves 4

1 tablespoon olive oil
1 large onion, finely chopped
1 garlic clove, finely chopped
2 teaspoons turmeric
1 teaspoon ground cumin
1 teaspoon ground cinnamon
200 g (7 oz) red lentils
salt and freshly ground black pepper
400 g (14 oz) spinach, washed
juice of ½ a lemon

Heat the oil in a large saucepan or casserole dish and cook the onion, garlic and spices over a low heat for 5 minutes.

Add the lentils and 1 litre (1¾ pints) of water and season lightly. Bring to the boil then reduce the heat and leave to simmer for around 30 minutes, stirring from time to time.

Meanwhile, wilt the spinach in a second saucepan in a little salted water. Once cooked, drain and set aside.

Once the lentils are cooked through, blend until smooth then add the spinach and blend roughly; you should still be able to see pieces of spinach.

Reheat gently if necessary, add the lemon juice and check the seasoning.

Indian-style split pea soup

Preparation time: 10 minutes
Cooking time: 35 minutes
Serves 8

2 tablespoons olive oil
1 large onion, finely chopped
1 garlic clove, finely chopped
1 teaspoon grated fresh root ginger
1 tablespoon ground coriander
1 teaspoon ground cumin
400 g (14 oz) dried yellow split
  peas (chana dahl)
250 g (8¾ oz) canned peeled
  tomatoes
salt and freshly ground black pepper
juice of a lemon
chopped fresh mint or coriander
  leaves, to garnish (optional)

Heat the oil in a large saucepan and cook the onion, garlic and ginger very gently for around 5 minutes until the onion is translucent.

Add the spices and brown for a few minutes.

Rinse the yellow split peas in cold water.

Reduce the heat to very low, add the split peas and tomatoes, stir well then add 1.75 litres (3 pints) of water. Stir again and season.

Bring to the boil and simmer for around 30 minutes, stirring occasionally, until the split peas are well cooked.

Remove from the heat, blend and add the lemon juice. Reheat gently if necessary and check the seasoning.

Before serving, sprinkle with freshly chopped mint or coriander, if using.

Seasonal vegetable soup

Preparation time: 15 minutes
Cooking time: 30 minutes
Serves 4

Winter version
1 large carrot, peeled and chopped
1 leek, chopped
¼–½ cabbage (green or white),
    chopped
1 onion, chopped
4–5 lettuce leaves, chopped
1 turnip, peeled and chopped
¼ pumpkin or 1 small squash,
    chopped
salt and freshly ground black pepper

Summer version
Replace the turnip with
    1 large courgette, chopped
Replace the pumpkin with
    1 large tomato

Place all the vegetables in a large heavy-based saucepan and add 1 litre (1¾ pints) of water. Season.

Leave to cook for 25–30 minutes, until all the vegetables are very soft (particularly the carrots).

Blend roughly so that the vegetables are still chunky.

Tips: This type of soup often appears in magazines as a 'fat-free soup'. Made without potato or any fat it is nonetheless a delicious, full-flavoured vegetable soup.

You could add a little milk or crème fraîche just before serving.

Forager's soup

Preparation time: 15 minutes
Cooking time: 30 minutes
Serves 6

1 tablespoon olive oil
2 shallots, finely chopped
300 g (10½ oz) young nettle shoots, washed
300 g (10½ oz) spinach, washed
125 g (4½ oz) sorrel leaves, washed
125 g (4½ oz) dandelion leaves, washed
3 potatoes, peeled and roughly chopped
salt and freshly ground black pepper
a pinch of grated nutmeg
100 ml (3½ fl oz) single cream

Heat the oil in a large lidded saucepan and cook the shallots over a low heat for around 5 minutes.

Add all the leaves and allow to wilt for a few minutes.

Add the potatoes and 1.5 litres (2¾ pints) of water. Season, cover and leave to cook over a medium heat for around 25 minutes.

Remove from the heat. Add the nutmeg and the cream. Blend until smooth, reheat gently if necessary and check the seasoning.

Tip: You can find tender nettles and dandelions in the spring. You could also replace them with watercress. The nettles are slightly acidic, the dandelions are a little bitter, watercress is a little smoother... The dandelions must be young and you should only pick the best ones. None of your greenery should be gathered near chemically treated crops.

Courgette soup with soft cheese

Preparation time: 10 minutes
Cooking time: 20 minutes
Serves 4

1 teaspoon olive oil
1 onion, sliced
3 spring onions, sliced
a pinch of ground cumin
4 courgettes, chopped
salt and freshly ground black pepper
8 soft cheese portions such
   as Dairylea

Heat the oil in a large saucepan and brown the onion and spring onions for a few minutes with the cumin.

Add the courgettes and 500–750 ml (18–26 fl oz) of water; the courgettes do not need to be completely covered by the water as they have a high water content. Season.

Cook over a low heat for around 15 minutes until the courgettes are soft.

Away from the heat, add most of the cheese and blend until smooth. Reheat gently if necessary, check the seasoning and serve dotted with the reserved cheese.

Tip: Before blending, set aside a little of the cooking water. The courgettes can make the soup a little too liquid. If necessary, you can add the water again while blending to get the texture you require.

Courgette and herb soup

Preparation time: 10 minutes
Cooking time: 15 minutes
Serves 6

1 kg (2 lb 4 oz) courgettes, chopped
3 spring onions, quartered
a good pinch of ground cumin
salt and freshly ground black pepper
3–4 sprigs of fresh tarragon, basil,
   mint or sage, plus extra to garnish
   (optional)
2 tablespoons single cream

Place the courgettes and spring onions in a large saucepan or casserole dish and add 500–750 ml (18–26 fl oz) of water; the courgettes do not need to be completely covered by the water as they have a high water content.

Add the cumin, season and cook over a low heat for around 15 minutes, until the courgettes are soft.

Away from the heat, add the tarragon, basil, mint or sage. Add the cream and blend until smooth. Reheat gently if necessary and check the seasoning. Garnish with extra herb sprigs, if using.

Tip: In the summer you could serve this soup lukewarm or even cold. The courgette makes the soup lovely and creamy and accentuates the flavours of the herbs.

Pea and mint soup

Preparation time: 20 minutes
Cooking time: 30 minutes
Serves 4

450 g (1 lb oz) peas (fresh or frozen)
1 lettuce heart or several leaves,
    chopped
3 spring onions or 1 large onion,
    chopped
salt and freshly ground black pepper
100 ml (3½ fl oz) single cream
3 sprigs of fresh mint

Place all the vegetables in a large heavy-based saucepan. Add 750 ml (26 fl oz) of water, season and bring to the boil. Reduce the heat and leave to simmer for 25 minutes.

Away from the heat, add the cream and mint. Blend until smooth.

Reheat gently if necessary, check the seasoning and serve.

Gazpacho

Preparation time: 30 minutes +
30 minutes chilling
Serves 8

1 cucumber, finely chopped
1 green or yellow pepper,
de-seeded and finely sliced
1.3 kg (2 lb 12 oz) tomatoes
  (fresh or canned), chopped
4 spring onions, finely chopped
2 garlic cloves, finely chopped
½ teaspoon caster sugar
3 tablespoons olive oil
3 tablespoons balsamic vinegar
salt and freshly ground black pepper
Tabasco sauce (optional)

Put all the vegetables into a large bowl. Add the garlic, sugar, oil and vinegar. Season.

Blend roughly, adding 200 ml (7 fl oz) of water to get a slightly more liquid consistency. It's good to leave a few crunchy pieces of cucumber and pepper.

Check the seasoning adding a little more vinegar if necessary and a few drops of Tabasco sauce if you wish.

Chill for at least half an hour before serving.

Four variations on gazpacho soup

Make the Gazpacho soup (see page 52) but with the variations as described below...

Gazpacho and avocado *(top left)*
Blend the gazpacho until smooth. Peel 2 avocados and chop into bite-sized chunks. Sprinkle each portion of soup with some of the avocado. You could add a little extra Tabasco sauce to counteract the sweetness of the avocado if wished.

Gazpacho and crab *(bottom left)*
Drain 2 cans of crabmeat, place in a small bowl and squeeze over the juice of ½ a lemon. Add to the bowls of soup just before serving.

Gazpacho and Feta *(top right)*
Crumble 100 g (3½ oz) of Feta cheese and sprinkle over the bowls of soup. Blend the soup with the Feta if you want it to be really smooth.

Gazpacho and hard boiled egg *(bottom right)*
For every 2 people being served, boil 1 egg for 10 minutes. Cut the boiled eggs into small pieces and sprinkle on the soup just before serving.

Iced Bloody Mary

Preparation time: 10 minutes +
5 hours chilling
Cooking time: 25 minutes
Serves 6

2 teaspoons olive oil
4 celery sticks, finely chopped
1.5 kg (3 lb 5 oz) ripe tomatoes (or
canned peeled tomatoes), peeled
and chopped
zest of ½ a lime
salt and freshly ground black pepper
100 ml (3½ fl oz) vodka (or to taste)
juice of 2 limes
1 tablespoon Tabasco sauce (or to
taste)
1 tablespoon Worcestershire sauce
ice, to serve

Heat the oil in a large lidded saucepan and cook the celery over a low heat for around 15 minutes, stirring regularly. It should be soft.

Add the tomatoes and lime zest. Season, cover and leave to simmer for 10 minutes.

Remove from the heat and blend until smooth.

Add the vodka, lime juice and Tabasco and Worcestershire sauce. You can alter the quantity of vodka and Tabasco according to taste.

Leave to cool then put in the fridge for at least 5 hours.

Serve very cold with ice cubes or crushed ice.

Cold carrot soup with pineapple and ginger

Preparation time: 20 minutes +
5 hours chilling
Cooking time: 35 minutes
Serves 6

1 teaspoon olive oil
2 onions, finely chopped
2 teaspoons fresh root ginger,
grated
1 kg (2 lb 4 oz) carrots, peeled
and sliced
salt and freshly ground black pepper
1 pineapple, peeled, cored and
cut into pieces
250 ml (9 fl oz) pineapple juice

Heat the oil in a large saucepan and soften the onions. Add the ginger and leave to cook for 5 minutes, stirring from time to time.

Add the carrots and 1 litre (1¾ pints) of water. Season. Bring to the boil then reduce the heat and leave to cook for around 30 minutes.

Once the carrots are soft, remove the soup from the heat and add the pineapple and juice. Blend, adding a little water if it is too thick. Season again if necessary.

Leave to cool then put in the fridge for at least 5 hours.

Cucumber 'milkshake' with fresh herbs

Preparation time: 10 minutes +
10 minutes chilling
Serves 5–6

1 cucumber, chopped
1 spring onion, finely chopped
750 ml (26 fl oz) semi skimmed
milk
250 g (8¾ oz) full fat natural yogurt
1 small bunch fresh herbs (mint,
coriander, basil, dill, etc.), chopped
salt and freshly ground black pepper

Blend together the cucumber, spring onion, milk, yogurt and herbs. Season.

Put in the fridge for 10 minutes and serve cold. Mix well before serving, ideally with a whisk to give it a really smooth milkshake texture.

Tip: This soup can be prepared in no time and is best made just before serving as this will give it a lighter texture.

Cold courgette, ginger and pickled lemon soup

Preparation time: 15 minutes +
  5 hours chilling
Cooking time: 20 minutes
Serves 6

1 tablespoon olive oil
2 onions, finely chopped
5 cm (2 inches) fresh root ginger,
  finely chopped
1 kg (2 lb 4 oz) courgettes, sliced
salt and freshly ground black pepper
1 pickled lemon in brine, finely
  sliced

Heat the oil in a large saucepan and cook the onions and ginger gently for around 5 minutes.

Add the courgettes and 500–750 ml (18–26 fl oz) of water; the courgettes do not need to be completely covered by the water as they have a high water content. Season.

Bring to the boil then reduce the heat and leave to cook for around 10 minutes or until the courgettes are soft.

Remove from the heat, blend until smooth and check the seasoning. Add the lemon.

Leave to cool then put in the fridge for at least 5 hours.

Tip: To be served really cold, this soup should be prepared at least half a day in advance.

Cold watermelon and Feta soup

Preparation time: 10 minutes +
1 hour chilling
Serves 4

1 large slice of watermelon, skin
  and seeds removed
juice of ½ a lemon
salt and freshly ground black pepper
1 small block of Feta cheese,
  crumbled
2 sprigs of fresh basil, chopped
  (optional)

Put the fruit in a blender and add the lemon juice. Season lightly.

Blend until smooth. Put in the fridge for at least 1 hour.

Sprinkle the soup with the cheese and basil, if using, and serve.

Cold peach and nectarine soup with mint

Preparation time: 15 minutes +
1 hour chilling
Serves 6

2 ripe peaches, stoned and chopped
2 ripe white peaches (see Tip),
stoned and chopped
2 ripe nectarines, stoned and
chopped
2 ripe white nectarines (see Tip),
stoned and chopped
leaves from 2 sprigs of fresh mint,
plus 1 whole sprig
icing sugar, to taste

Blend together all the ingredients (except the whole mint sprig) with a little iced water. Alter how much water you add depending on the desired consistency of the soup. A thick rough soup will resemble a fruit compote; adding more liquid will make the soup more like a smoothie. Add a little icing sugar to taste if necessary.

Chill in the fridge for 1 hour. Decorate with the remaining mint leaves just before serving.

Tip: If you can't find white peaches and nectarines, use normal ones instead.

Nectarine and raspberry soup

Preparation time: 10 minutes +
   1 hour chilling
Serves 4–5

6 very ripe nectarines, chopped
juice of a lemon
300 g (10½ oz) raspberries
icing sugar, to taste
2 sprigs of fresh basil (optional),
   chopped

Sprinkle the nectarines with the lemon juice.

Rinse the raspberries and set aside one-third for decoration.

Blend together all the fruit (except the reserved raspberries) with a little icing sugar if necessary.

Chill in the fridge for 1 hour. Decorate with the remaining raspberries and the chopped basil, if using, just before serving.

Tip: You could make this soup with peaches instead of nectarines, but peel them before chopping.

Spiced cream of carrot and coconut soup

Preparation time: 30 minutes +
  1 hour chilling
Cooking time: 30 minutes
Serves 6

300 g (10½ oz) carrots, peeled
  and sliced
150 ml (5 fl oz) milk
½ teaspoon ground coriander
1 teaspoon ground cinnamon
4 pinches of nutmeg
100 ml (3½ fl oz) coconut milk
150 ml (5 fl oz) condensed milk
a few drops of vanilla extract
20 g (¾ oz) desiccated coconut

Place the carrots in a large saucepan with 150 ml (5 fl oz) of water and the milk, coriander, cinnamon and nutmeg. Cook for 30 minutes over a low heat until the carrots are soft. Add a little extra water during cooking if necessary.

Away from the heat, add the coconut milk, condensed milk and vanilla extract and blend until smooth. The soup should have a creamy consistency.

Add the desiccated coconut and stir in. Chill in the fridge for at least 1 hour.

Note: This recipe was invented by my cook, Fritz Talvin. He makes an excellent carrot and coconut soup and wanted to push the idea to its extreme and make a sweet version. This creamy soup is absolutely delicious. It reminds me of those slightly mysterious Indian desserts that are also made with a carrot base.

Index

Conversion tables

The tables below are only approximate and are meant to be used as a guide only.

Approximate American/ European conversions

	USA	Metric	Imperial
brown sugar	1 cup	170 g	6 oz
butter	1 stick	115 g	4 oz
butter/ margarine/ lard	1 cup	225 g	8 oz
caster and granulated sugar	2 level tablespoons	30 g	1 oz
caster and granulated sugar	1 cup	225 g	8 oz
currants	1 cup	140 g	5 oz
flour	1 cup	140 g	5 oz
golden syrup	1 cup	350 g	12 oz
ground almonds	1 cup	115 g	4 oz
sultanas/ raisins	1 cup	200 g	7 oz

Approximate American/ European conversions

American	European
1 teaspoon	1 teaspoon/ 5 ml
½ fl oz	1 tablespoon/ ½ fl oz/ 15 ml
¼ cup	4 tablespoons/ 2 fl oz/ 50 ml
½ cup plus 2 tablespoons	¼ pint/ 5 fl oz/ 150 ml
1¼ cups	½ pint/ 10 fl oz/ 300 ml
1 pint/ 16 fl oz	1 pint/ 20 fl oz/ 600 ml
2½ pints (5 cups)	1.2 litres/ 2 pints
10 pints	4.5 litres/ 8 pints

Liquid measures

Imperial	ml	fl oz
1 teaspoon	5	
2 tablespoons	30	
4 tablespoons	60	
¼ pint/ 1 gill	150	5
⅓ pint	200	7
½ pint	300	10
¾ pint	425	15
1 pint	600	20
1¾ pints	1000 (1 litre)	35

Oven temperatures

American	Celsius	Fahrenheit	Gas Mark
Cool	130	250	½
Very slow	140	275	1
Slow	150	300	2
Moderate	160	320	3
Moderate	180	350	4
Moderately hot	190	375	5
Fairly hot	200	400	6
Hot	220	425	7
Very hot	230	450	8
Extremely hot	240	475	9

Other useful measurements

Measurement	Metric	Imperial
1 American cup	225 ml	8 fl oz
1 egg, size 3	50 ml	2 fl oz
1 egg white	30 ml	1 fl oz
1 rounded tablespoon flour	30 g	1 oz
1 rounded tablespoon cornflour	30 g	1 oz
1 rounded tablespoon caster sugar	30 g	1 oz
2 level teaspoons gelatine	10 g	¼ oz